U.S. SYMBOLS
THE STATUE OF LIBERTY

by Tyler Monroe

Consulting Editor: Gail Saunders-Smith, PhD

CAPSTONE PRESS
a capstone imprint

Pebble Plus is published by Capstone Press,
1710 Roe Crest Drive, North Mankato, Minnesota 56003
www.capstonepub.com

Library of Congress Cataloging-in-Publication Data
Monroe, Tyler, 1976–
 The Statue of Liberty / by Tyler Monroe.
   pages cm.—(Pebble plus. U.S. symbols)
 Includes bibliographical references and index.
 Summary: "Simple text and full-color photographs briefly describe The Statue of Liberty and its role as a national
symbol"—Provided by publisher.
 Audience: Grades K-3.
 ISBN 978-1-4765-3088-8 (library binding)—ISBN 978-1-4765-3510-4 (ebook pdf)—ISBN 978-1-4765-3537-1 (pbk.)
 1. Statue of Liberty (New York, N.Y.)—History—Juvenile literature. 2. New York (N.Y.)—Buildings, structures, etc.—
Juvenile literature. I. Title.
 F128.64.L6M645 2014
 974.7'1—dc23   2013001825

Editorial Credits
Erika L. Shores, editor; Lori Bye, designer; Svetlana Zhurkin, media researcher; Eric Mankse, production specialist

Photo Credits
Alamy: North Wind Picture Archives, 11, 15; Corbis: Bettmann, 17; Library of Congress, 10, 13, 19; Shutterstock: Amy Nichole
Harris, cover, 7, DanielW, 1, ErickN, 5, iofoto, 9, Suat Gursozlu (stars), cover and throughout, Yuri Arcurs, 21

Note to Parents and Teachers

The U.S. Symbols set supports national social studies standards related to people, places, and
culture. This book describes and illustrates the Statue of Liberty. The images support early readers
in understanding the text. The repetition of words and phrases helps early readers learn new words.
This book also introduces early readers to subject-specific vocabulary words, which are defined in
the Glossary section. Early readers may need assistance to read some words and to use the Table of
Contents, Glossary, Read More, Internet Sites, and Index sections of the book.

Printed in China by Nordica.
0314/CA21400181
022014   007226NORDF13

TABLE OF CONTENTS

A National Symbol

The Statue of Liberty is a symbol

of American freedom.

The statue is of a woman

holding a tablet and a torch.

The torch and tablet stand for different things. The torch means she is bringing the light of freedom to the world. The tablet stands for the United States' laws.

The statue is on Liberty Island

in New York Harbor. The statue

is made of steel and copper.

The torch towers more than 300 feet

(91 meters) above the ground.

A Gift from France

France gave the Statue of

Liberty to the United States.

It was a gift of friendship.

The statue was designed

by Frédéric Auguste Bartholdi.

Frédéric Auguste Bartholdi

Workers began building
the statue in Paris, France,
in 1875. It was ready to send
to the United States in 1884.

13

The statue was too big to send
in one piece. Workers took it
apart and shipped it in 214 crates.
The statue and the base it stands
on were finished in 1886.

15

The Symbol Then and Now

For many years, immigrants came to America by ship. The ships passed the Statue of Liberty. The statue welcomed people to the United States.

Over time weather hurt the
Statue of Liberty. By the 1980s
repairs were needed. The statue
was cleaned inside and out.
A new torch was made.

19

Millions of people visit the

Statue of Liberty each year.

Visitors go inside the statue.

They can climb 354 steps to look

out of the crown on her head.

Glossary

copper—a red-brown metal; copper turns green from the air and weather

design—to make a plan for how to make something

freedom—the right to live the way you want

harbor—a place where ships can stay safe from storms

immigrant—a person who leaves one country and makes a home in another

repairs—the action of fixing something

symbol—an object that stands for something else

tablet—a pad of writing paper

torch—a flaming light

Read More

Behrens, Janice. *What Is the Statue of Liberty?* Scholastic News Nonfiction Readers. New York: Children's Press, 2009.

Harris, Nancy. *The Statue of Liberty.* Patriotic Symbols. Chicago: Heinemann Library, 2008.

Moriarty, Siobhan. *Visit the Statue of Liberty.* Landmarks of Liberty. New York: Gareth Stevens Pub., 2012.

Internet Sites

FactHound offers a safe, fun way to find Internet sites related to this book. All of the sites on FactHound have been researched by our staff.

Here's all you do:

Visit *www.facthound.com*

Type in this code: 9781476530888

Super-cool stuff! Check out projects, games and lots more at **www.capstonekids.com**

23

Critical Thinking Using Common the Core

1. Why are the torch and the tablet important parts of the Statue of Liberty? (Key Ideas and Details)

2. Why do you think immigrants felt welcomed by the Statue of Liberty? (Key Ideas and Details)

3. The Statue of Liberty is a symbol of freedom. What does freedom mean? (Craft and Structure)

Index

Word Count: 237
Grade: 1
Early-Intervention Level: 23

24